FROM HOOD TO MAN

"Letters To Self"

Written by
Grinell Tyson Jr.

© 2018 Grinell Tyson
ISBN# 9780692184080

LCCN# 2018910694

All rights reserved. Without limiting the rights under copyright reserved above. No part of this book may be reproduced, stored in or introduced into a retrieval system, or transmitted in any form, or by any means (electronic, mechanical, photocopying, recording, or otherwise) without prior written consent from the author except brief quotes used in reviews, interviews or magazines. This is a work of fiction. It is not meant to depict, portray or represent any particular real person. All the characters, incidents and dialogue in this written work are the product of the author's imagination and are not to be considered as real. Any references or similarities to actual events, entities, real people living or dead, or to real locations are intended for the sole purpose of giving this novel a sense of reality. Any similarities with other names, characters, entities, places, people or incidents are entirely coincidental.

Dedication:

To my young KING Grinell Tyson 3rd

Rest In Paradise Tony V. Duhart

To My Brother From Another (Richard)
I Love You And You Will Forever Be Missed. I'm Sorry Sometimes Change Doesn't Add Up To What We Always Hope!

Acknowledgments

I first want to thank everyone who stood up for me and with me through these times I write about and every other time I did not mention due to circumstances. Ms. Gerwin, Mrs. Parker, and Ms. Tammy; you strong women stood by me through so much. Not the fact that it was your job, y'all did above and beyond. I will always love y'all heart. Thank you! To my child's mom, you are strength and hope and don't even know it. Thanks, a trillion woman. I want to definitely also thank my parents for doing what you could even through the storm. Glad such courageous and mighty people had this blessing that stands tall today! Thank you to all the people that spread their greatness upon me and let me in doors I could only dream of ....

A Word from the Author

It's time to start and start now! Start what you ask? Well my people, I'm asking you to read this with a steady eye and (I)!...This is the self-knowledge I've gained growing up in the streets of Toledo Ohio and now I have become an open book in hopes of penetrating your mind and opening up your consciousness to some of the hostile and beautiful realities that I have discovered. If I may be blunt; I am the product of a home with values that lay in the middle of the street in a lot of cases. As I write this, I hate to cast such an extreme shadow of craziness on my family and home life, but I must honestly state the truth of what I witnessed and experienced.

How to love one self and how to treat life and others begins in the home. These and more are learned from the home, which if not properly structured, will only bring destruction in all forms. I would like to welcome you; the readers and non-believers, into my collection of insights which I've acquired through experience, absorbing information, and observing the old and new walks of my life! Again, I'm asking you to inhale my words with pure peace and allow them to become rooted inside you; so much so that it chills your very soul! I thank you for taking the time to delve into my journey of self-education, self-discovery, and the exploration of what I see as major hindrances to progression in my community!

TABLE OF CONTENTS

FROM HOOD TO MAN i
Table of Contents 7
Introduction 10
I Hear You Tyson: The Beginning of Destruction and Conquer 12
The Struggle of Man 18
What Lifestyle Leads Up To: 19
Why I've Changed 21
The ABILITY TO LIVE LIFE SKILLFULLY 23
Am I Surviving Oppression/Trauma 28
The Day I Lived and Died 34
Displacement 36
Grind Time 40
Blinding Oppression 42
Battle Lines 48
Coming For You 51
I See 54
Recovery 57
Where I Come From 59
Step Inside: Conscious 62
True-Man 63

Listen Up! Another Gun   64
Respect & Understand   65
I-am   67
THE PAIN OF HOOD 69
"HOME"   70
"Strength Hope Faith"   72
"READY"   74
"BEAUTIFUL TRAuMA"   76
"Reality"   78
"THOUGHTS AND PRAYERS"   80
"TIME IS SUICIDE"   81
"unknown"   83
"I DON'T KNOW"   85
"I WANT" 87
Struggle   89
UNMANAGEABLE   90
"1 Story"   92
A Beautiful Pain 93
"A Pray for Love"   94
"For Prayers of Love" 2   95
"Sister In Mind" 96
"Deep seeking of destiny" 97
"One places intransigent through the perception of ignorance"   99
"Please Just Stop"   101
"Understand"   102
"Why he hug deem streets"   103
A Good Man   105
"Wise to Know" 107

"A BOY's ISSUES"   108
"BELIEVE ME"   110
"Conquer Man Conquer Beast"   111
"Drunk Mind"   112
"A Dry Why"   114
"EMOTIONS" 118
"Eye 2 C"   119
"EYE OF MY GHETTO"   121
"I Can't"   123
"I'm Lord"   124
"FATE"   126
"Lost #1"   127
"Never Stop" 128
"ONLY YOU CAN"   129
"Seek In Self"   130
"Silence in the cell" 132
"Taking Her Love"   134
"THANK YOU FAMILY" 135
"THE GREATEST CARE"   136
"Till I Die"   138
"Too Many Chances"   139
"Unique"   141
"WHY THIS"   142
"You're my Faith"   143
"EYE SEE"   144
"SEND OFF"   145
Apologetic flipped was switched   146
Take These Tips That I Lend With All My love: 150
LAST WORDS 152

INTRODUCTION

I am Grinell Tyson Jr. and I would like for my readers to fully grasp the fundamental nature of who I am. My life experiences consist of mental health challenges, alcoholism and drug addiction; to say my family dynamics were dysfunctional is in my opinion an understatement. I was a product of a street life that consisted of gang involvement and many different criminal acts, ranging from disorderly conduct and menacing to felonies such as burglary, robbery and gun charges. I have battled depression and suicidal ideations many times in my life. I've struggled throughout my life asking what is wrong with me and why am I like this? I have lost friends and family to gun violence, domestic violence and AIDS. I have been kicked out of more schools than I can count. Violence seemed to be preferred and normal behavior in my childhood. I have many siblings from different Moms and one Dad; some of which I have never met. My grandmother was put to rest when I was a child. After losing her, life became a blur for me. I spent many nights in jail as a juvenile and went to prison once I reached adulthood. I spent years and nights fighting bad memories to the point of continual insomnia; I did my best to sleep during the day. I come from a single parent home that included roaches and rats. At a very young age I experienced being homeless, literally out in the streets with no one to answer to. This is me, GRINELL TYSON JR.; this is the crux of it, and yes there's much more about me that I have yet to disclose and if you continue, you'll discover more of me in the following pages. This intro exists to give my readers a clear understanding of who their writer *was* and *is* as a person, and particularly for those of you who may share a similar story. I want you to know that change is scary and it's hard, but it's what defines the true you and IT IS POSSIBLE! So, know you are worth more and you can make it with the right amount of strength, structure, sacrifice and most importantly the vision to see and believe...have FAITH.

I HEAR YOU TYSON: THE BEGINNING OF DESTRUCTION AND CONQUER

This is to the ones who watched my pain; who only had so many words but acted as though they understood. I have been going through this life struggling for so long; hoping to get nothing but love, hugs and praying for true support and loyalty to be my final drug. I was raised by parents who were love struck, but understanding wasn't the brightest when it came to a child's touch.

Many nights I sit up hearing the loud music and partying. Right before the fighting started, I would be thinking about going to school for escape, only to get there and vent with active rage and hate, and then go home. I'd be surrounded by a life beyond just crime and crazy. I would sit playing with bullets as if they were a new toy. I enjoyed them lying there. I was playing with weed like I was one of the cool adults. I was always sitting on my Grandma's porch as drugs went into the vent and money was being laundered and spent. I got to watch everything being sold that was just stole, to the shoot outs that seemed to last too long. When I went down to my friend's house, I couldn't help wanting his toys; couldn't wait til' him and his Dad left, so me, Cuz, and Sister could get in that window and enjoy.

We would play with the crack heads, shitty Billy and white Joe.

"Hey Meechie, bet I can hit him harder with a canned good than you!"

Crazy to say, I was only 9 soon to be 10 and ready to find my first gun. This was not the first time I'd seen one.

Aunty's house had everything in it but a couch; she didn't even clean, only when the white people come over to check on the kids. It was like nothing was left in the world when Grandma passed. I knew it was gone be bad when everyone went crazy in the hospital, but if you ask me, she was kept from her home!

Yeah, that's the reason why, but who am I to say? Coming from a young eye, that was no different from Aunty starving little cousin, making him eat out the garbage like some dog. Well, I couldn't judge, it was probably worse watching Daddy stump 11-year-old

Sister on that hill like some thug. Maybe that's why Big Sis runs away. Is that really her Dad? Yup, the guy that walks around all crazy like he on something. Well, no one speaks on it much, so it was probably best to leave it alone. I saw that freezer full of money Momma was counting with them guys that come to our house. I wonder if that's how we get to go to all those car shows. It's fun!

It's better than when all these girls start touching on me and I keep telling them how bad it hurts. I want to say something but I always think that everybody's just gonna laugh. I don't know if it's worse than Daddy drinking that stuff with all his friends, then later chasing Momma in the car because he's mad. At least that was better than when he used to scare me, never knowing if he was going to be happy or sad drinking that stuff. I used to think he was showing out; he makes me hate this place.

I wonder is that stuff the reason why he keeps trying to hurt himself and then we have to go see him in that hospital place.

If I was Sis, I would run away or jump out my bedroom window too, even though I didn't like that one night she made me leave with her. I knew something wasn't right. I still wonder how everything got so split up? Precious going to live somewhere on the north,

Nanny in the Ville and me left with myself, not even knowing properly how to live.

What is a child to do? I'm barely past 13 now and I have a house to myself, wondering why juvenile detention and the projects keep becoming my home of homes. Falling in love with all the love of the friends that seem to have been where I am and are helping me survive; they become more like family than friends.

I'm getting older and trying to get to the money with no regrets.

I'm saying, "Forget school till I get me some better shoes, praying no one notices these three pair of pants I keep having to wear! Shoot.... Daddy won't let me wear his".

"What's up Tyson, I'm Violence."

"What's up Violence, I'm Tyson!"

Yup, this is the introduction that flipped it for me. As crazy and backwards as it sounds, it helps me, unconsciously, I never even care or want to hide it. Walking the streets while my mother and my dad somewhere lying in bed, appearing to me to be in pure peace.

I'm 17 sleeping in the park, not allowing a shower to stop my start; I'm in love with the only thing I know, which is the gutter like none other. From booming rocks to stopping clocks, I feel the need. I have no worries. I think I'm a man, but the truth is I'm really not; I'm having sex with plenty women, staying with many and not even 18, but chillin' all through the city.

See, I'm ready, but am I? I never knew truly what it meant to break an issue down, all I know is I'm no longer swimming; somewhere along the way, I began to drown. See, I knew my death was coming back at age 16 and nothing was going to be able to stop it. They see I'm not in school, and when I'm present breaking all the rules; rebellious as they come, so they just labeled me as dumb; all the while not understanding where this child comes from.

In first grade, I loved school and I knew it was cool. I guess black can only be fixed one way; when you're only looking out of one eye. Now I soon will drown because the pills and Special Ed classes couldn't fix the kid. All my teachers told me in elementary that only death and jail would be my home.

Now my people, how did this happen? The young man getting shipped off to be a ward of the state, facing a prison sentence close to seven years. What happened to the death at 16? How come such chaos is happening? How did he even get the gun? Where could this have even begun? Only more pain is my heart going to feel and at the end, once again they will say he had a way; that's his deal. Well sorry for them, I did the "unnorm" as they perceive and picked up a book. Will that be the end of my pain or will there be more to face? Well I say no, I doubt it, it wont be more pain because I'm going into a new lane that should fight for my pain and the pain of others, but we'll see……

THE STRUGGLE OF MAN

WHAT LIFESTYLE LEADS UP TO:

"People need to understand you give the maximum risk to jeopardize your freedom or life by lacking knowledge when it comes to information". We must start taking control of the issues we have and emotions we feel from time to time because with unresolved issues, we began to allow them to control our thinking; which leads us to an unconscious lifestyle. We must realize and understand life is what we make it and once we create the forum, we create our own style. It is now placed in real life settings. Understanding plus studying this knowledge of lifestyle, helps us from being: blind, deaf, and dumb to what's happening to us. Why struggle or fight to keep what you have!

(WHAT LIFESTYLE LEADS UP TO)

Actual Journal Entry Solitary Confinement at S.O.C.F (LUCASVILLE) Correctional Facility

2012

"I remember sitting in my cell thinking how I ended up here!"

WHY I'VE CHANGED

As I sat in prison doing over 6 years, I had a vision of what it would be like to think for myself. Slowly but surely, I was learning how to think things through fully before applying action. I began seeing myself as a young boy, who sat in a man's structure as an aggressive, selfish and stubborn individual; seeing nothing but the machine he was forced to live through. I watched, sometimes helplessly as life passed me by.

Speaking to a person one day and then hearing the next day they're dead and gone began to overtake my head space. Family and friends, some who were the same age as I was, were dying off and I couldn't even view a body or physically pay my respect.

I went to max security my last 3 years in prison, sitting in a cell 24 hours a day, 23 on some, and later 21 hours. I remember rubbing my ankles from the shackles most nights while listening to the voices and the loudness of the bars; most importantly the overall cowardice. I never imagined experiencing such a sight and situation in my life. My awareness heightened, and I was beginning to think so clearly, yet I was in an environment where chaos and torment permeated every inch of that place. I came to describe it as being "insane inside of being sane." I was being fed through bars like an animal while just around the corner from me in the same prison, a man was literally about to take his last breath *or* a man's life was being taken away.

    I sat alone with my walls, seeing the love my family and so-called friends had to give. I began reading and studying daily. I was learning how information provided you access to all success in life. From learning all about the good and bad habits of humans, maintaining financially, to living life comfortably without having to watch your back. I began to learn the word humbleness, everybody doesn't have to react; we all have a choice. I stopped being blind to so much in life. Either you're going to properly break the issue down or you're going to let your issues control you and run your life while you sit back and feel the effects from what unresolved issues could do to your life. I learned that the actions I take in my life result in consequences that could turn into someone else's pain that does not deserve it. I truly had to learn how I was a human first, a person, and then a man.

THE ABILITY TO LIVE LIFE SKILLFULLY

"I" is self, never get lost in thy EYE!

"Apply your heart to instruction and your ears to words of knowledge". 23:12 "Tune your ears to wisdom and concentrate on understanding" 2:2 nlt "Make your ear attentive to wisdom, Incline your heart to understanding" 2:2 nasb..."incline thine ear unto wisdom, and apply thine heart to understanding" 2:2 kjv are Proverbs to take seriously in this day and age. We as people sometimes cause harm to ourselves by ruining our own image and damaging the ones we love! Me? I was a prime example of the kind of person that would cause such devastation due to ignorance about myself and about life.

When I discovered what I call "self-inside of life," I learned that I was *conscious in chaos*; I was becoming aware of my reason for living and the colossal goals that I wanted to achieve all while fighting to reshape my mind and shed the life I was used to. That was the only life I knew but one that did not groom me for an abundant life. People grow up with particular core values and a level of self-worth that is shaped from within, and more often than not, it's attributed to our environment the particular lifestyles that we were exposed to. Of course, it's not because we asked for it, but being youngsters who are vulnerable with limited control, we're ultimately left with no choice but to endure our given circumstances. We are pretty much at the mercy of those who are expected to prepare us for adulthood. Even the ones who loved us the most only flinched at our screams of "please help" and "I need sense of direction."

After so long, we grasped our own perceptions; never truly acquiring the wisdom that is vital to maintaining and succeeding. With the lack of guidance and the poor examples placed before us by adults who exhibited mental and emotional deficiencies, our ill-equipped hearts and minds drifted off into a world where we are expected to handle life only to end up defeated, lost, and confused. Our values lay at an "eye" point of view and not the "I" point of view, which is what matters. I'd like to break down my learning of self to all those near and far. It's all about "I" point of "abuse" in all forms. Some should know that "visual abuse" (the continual witnessing of criminal and/or deviant behavior that severely alters one's mind and sensibilities to coexisting with others on a healthy level) is an equal part and less thought of form of abuse along with verbal and physical abuse.

Most people will refuse the notion that their negative behavior is even considered abuse and cannot see the seriousness of it because there is no "physical contact." Most of the time because the poisonous behavior is so engrained in us it overrides our conscience of knowing something is wrong or unhealthy. Over time, it dulls our senses to what we clearly see is destroying us and those around us! As we increase these habits of character, they become our basic people skills and eye of life. No matter how clear, pretty, or ugly the picture in front of us may be, we produce our basics. As we grow into adults, we may become wiser and grow tremendously in our own understanding and go far in our life, but some, if not all of our basic skills and values learned early in life keep a grip on our character. To rise up we have to deal with these head on. It's humbling when I think about the fact that not only did I have so much to discover about life; I've come to learn that there is so much about me that I didn't know!

As I reflect these quotes come to mind: "Hardest thing for someone to see is their self."

"It's hard for people to step away from their logic and say I'm going to step back and do something new."

"We all probably know it sometimes looks darkest before the dawn."

"The mind and life see it like a well, if you poison it and keep drinking from it, you'll soon die."

"Nothing you've been through will be wasted."

I heard these and said, "Whew! Thank you."

It is part of my duty not to waste these words. I do my best to stay "thorough" in my thinking, speaking, behavior, and the receiving of information! These things were not shaped in my childhood, at least not properly, and I realize I may always have the scars from my past. It's up to me to engage and implement these discoveries in my new life. I believe everything we've been through is or should have been serious lessons learned. Now that we have obtained new skills and information, we are the teachers that must look inward and grade ourselves on what we've learned up to this point. This is my insight on life for my past and present behavior, and how I found a sense of understanding to structuring my life for success. My entire life was practically tied up in destruction and I understand that the process of maintaining the man I am today will be a lifelong undertaking. When wisdom speaks, I'm more attentive and because I know better, I will do better. I know confidence has to always be in the "I" with first rate determination. I will live up to my fullest potential. I will use everything I've learned, allowing it to go deep and work to project it externally. I will cherish each moment in this life that I have been given.

Now, I close my eyes to pray and say "Thank You Consciousness for storing me with firm understanding and giving me such an amazing understanding of Consciousness. Amen!"

Sincerely, Grinell Tyson Jr.

Wrote in the Darkness of Lucasville Correctional Facility cell

*When I say, "(I) is self never get lost from thy eye." (eye), means sight; and sometimes we as individuals get lost from the sight in front of us instead of going with one's true self and our thoughts and feelings. (I) to me is the mental; it being CONSCIOUS (AWARE) OF SELF AND SELF INSIDE OF LIFE!

AM I SURVIVING OPPRESSION?

  I have found myself in numerous situations in *"my life"* and *"this life."* I make a distinction between the two because I have had to survive in the life seen by those around me, yet I held on to my own reality that I walked in alone; a reality that was not always visible to others. Over time, I discovered that I was feeling my way through another reality that had been fed to me by the powers that be. How do so many people who stand in supremacy watch as so many souls' burn and parents scream? How does money take precedence over someone being able to live and barely survive? I am shocked at the reality of consciousness having to become free from a trapped mind to see the harsh reality of insanity. To find out the A students [higher class, privileged citizens who are far removed from my hood] have no compassion for or understanding of those less privileged. How is it possible for someone to see another person burning and say they shouldn't have slipped in gas and fell on a lit cigarette? Why not ask how did the gas appear and who had the cigarette that would create such torturous episode. I have witnessed and lived through some moments like this scenario and I'm thankful to have survived. These harsh realities will cause you to grow up guarded on 24/7 survival mode; so much so that you protect yourself even in a simple conversation. You scrutinize and examine the words (even positive ones) of everyone, any and everything THAT matters.

As I write this, I'm twenty-five years old; I'm gaining knowledge and a self-awareness that is beginning to help me see the harsh reality of bloodshed being spread through all communities. Nothing but a false outlook is the response and the fake calling of we're on our way. Death is close and far how I grew up. I hate to see these onlookers saying they understand a child's pain or blaming them as if they had power over the poor value system people modeled for them. They have power over the words they always heard. To judge is to hate self. I use h-a-t-e as "having attitude towards everything."

I grew up never knowing or understanding the depths of words such as wisdom, morals, values, character, self, or structure. Positions of power, money source and self-preservation are more important than people in the urban community who live through cycles of all kinds of unimaginable abuse. To witness the agony of these souls up close and personal, on a daily basis, one must have a firm foundation of who they are and must be wise enough to understand that the conditions of life vary and will not always be fair or a pretty sight. How can one have such thoughts when emotion is a word only used through a broken school system? This world is a blessing of a curse for some and if some don't soon become aware, how will we ever survive the new times of new century oppression? [schools down, more prisons, more guns flooding the street *and* felons penalized. This is all oppression!]

Free Writing By 1 Love 2 Many Struggles

Sincerely Grinell Tyson Jr.

TRAUMA

The conditions of one's environment can be critical to the offspring. From an early age, I found myself having to utilize many survival tactics that should never have to be instilled in one so young.

After reflecting on my own journey through the trenches, I now wonder about how many other kids who are having to deal with the chaos of living, loyalty, and love. Many people watched my screams and I can't help but compassionately consider the young souls that are screaming out and being ignored at this very moment. Some say in the field I work in we need experience; however, as I sit alone in the corner [office], I can't help but to question if they understand this *experience* they're speaking of. [As an advocate, help them rise above stereotypes to their potential].

Definitely I agree, just wanting once again, pure enough to touch these communities' greatness or just enough to calm down the storm. I would love for the faces of those in need to leave my mental, for the voices of despair to cast away, and then again, I would love just to sleep peacefully. For me, my family and others. I can agree that these streets are getting out of control and almost beyond reach in some ways and it hurt sometimes. People take it seriously, but not enough to sit in it and get a front row seat and demand children and elders get the respect they deserve. [Wanting to genuinely help but sitting across from people who are clueless or don't care about the trauma of my people no outreach] added to my mental torture and led to depression.

This sort of trauma can send a man to the edge of self-destruction; the kind of destruction that will become his best and possibly his only teacher. Since no one is brave enough to speak up, I'll ask. Can someone come and save my people? And who are "my people", you ask? My people are all those who feel left out, those who think there is no other way; the ones who were pregnant at 13, but the family covered it up because that's what we do. My people are the ones suffering from mental health issues and addiction. They are blind to the fact that the first people skills they were handed to value was nothing but self-abuse, which grew to neglecting their entire environment and everything in existence that don't deserve such.

They say, "you can't save someone who doesn't want to be saved." Well I'm here to say THANK YOU Ms. Gerwin, Mrs. Parker, and Ms. Tammy because I was that young lost fool, ignorant to life and self, that had no intention of making it nowhere but prison or the grave and had no problem with either. I've been told to "look at someone and picture what that person can become; if you see them under a bridge, then envision them in a suit and tie recreating bridges for the world to see; and if your mind can't envision such greatness, I ask for the sake and mercy of my people, just let it be and leave it to the next who not only can see, but care enough to put that work in."

I understand their trauma because of my own.

See, all is needed when one is lost and subjected to the same garbage day in and day out. If you feed one such long enough and say it is steak, after so long I may just accept it as steak and be willing to neglect everything and put my life on the line for it. Have you ever been so far inside of abuse that you never even noticed or just became numb? Well, just don't judge mine. Uplift them 'cause it's enough judgment to go around. Can't you tell they're good at judging each other enough. Haven't you noticed the gun violence?

THE DAY I LIVED AND DIED

I pulled up... bang! bang!
Yeah! that's the way you ride!
Another day but a better day 'cause I shattered the way,
I swear the understanding of this barrel... is glory of love in my soul,
no question I been missing this stuff my whole life,
The passion and care it sends through my veins...bang! bang! this mutha even screams my name......
I swear my heart has a new beat that don't even know me,
but FORGET it I rather ignore it and cut it,
I'm now inspired to be inspired,
in my veins I feel many desires,
like my heart on fire or getting pulled through my back,
I must have been blessed with two hearts;
either that or the body has just created a new part,

I am a struggle...
I live with no muzzle,
I'm all over the place like a fresh puzzle,
I must be taken seriously...
or you may not survive well around me,
seriously!
Yeah, I'm 'bout that life and it's all about me,
even if it's not foreseeable to you,
you better make it easy to see,
I'm done being played with...... promise!
I was taught by struggle to bust this mutha quick!
Ain't playing just saying what's needed
cause I know chaos could balance with reason,
There is no love lost...... Maybe when this banger go off!

Free Writing By 1 Love 2 Many Struggles
Sincerely Grinell Tyson Jr.

DISPLACEMENT

I work in a field that requires the shaming or neglect of another to gain self-gratification in the areas of obtaining a title, pride, money, and power. The field of work I'm in is believed to do any and everything to help the less fortunate and provide individuals and families with the resources needed to build more stable communities. The grim reality is that it exists under disguise of humanitarianism and support, but underneath it there is a dark and convoluted side not seen by those on the outside looking in. Social work is to be social! Organizations are to be planted on fertile ground with seeds of compassion, integrity, and transparency so only that which is good can grow from it! Any organization claiming to be for the communities in which they occupy should strive to be rooted in the greatness of serving and not in the greatness of themselves. Somewhere along the way, many people have lost sight of what social work is about or it could be that they never had it to begin with. The dollar makes these agencies far from great and more for escape of mission and vision statements posted on the wall. They have drifted so far from them and the real work that needs to be done to nothingness in spirit. There is no genuine help. They know they're a dollar sign from human being to currency. How inhumane does one become or how much does one have to acquire or gain to reach the point of arrival where they forget the purpose and blessing that comes with being in this line of work? What does one have to acquire to improperly connect to the blessing this work field put us in line for? Shame on any man or woman who forgot what it is like to need a helping hand or are close minded to figuring out.

 I watch my culture in this field become an abomination to a young man, such as myself, who needs far from that. Where are the parents?

 I would have to answer, "Somewhere being obtuse in a corner with a broken soul."

 I ask where are the people who stepped up to be leaders to these broken spirits and lost souls? I can care less if it's the person in the mail room. Know who you are mailing for, step the heck up! What happened to treat one how we would want one to treat us? You know, do unto others, remember that? And if you do not care about how you are treated then know that is where the problems lay. Where is this madness coming from? This anger/ugliness? You people are the spirit of a fool. If you feel left out, it's probably because you are not seeing the door open for you.

I see this as disrespectful coming from a man who has been in the system; this system of so-called freedom and equal justice! As a man with a struggle and not only that, who is pushing to add greatness in his life with no disabilities, I guess that's not good enough!

Fake the depression. A lot of people have lost so much sight on greatness, on youth, and just remembering their first toy. Where is the heart? We see where the love truly is. Let's all not get to the top of the mountain and say things are just different up here. You can't move how you like, but in the same breath it's about getting the people to the top. We do what we can, as well as fight for what we want. These men and women have become the most cravenly imbeciles I've ever seen, and I spent years in the jungle. I still take looks on a daily and I balance the ignorance while at the same time, I balance the wise! And still the wise out shine with terrible results.

1love, Too Many Struggles
Sincerely,
Grinell Tyson Jr.

*I was working with people who I had great respect for at the time. To hear their comments about clients and people who they're suppose to sit and help made my blood boil. So, unlike what they said about people like me where I came from, I did the opposite and wrote about it. So, to those people, we do not all need to die or are just stupid'.... yes we do learn and grow.

GRIND TIME

I speak loud to my people, proud to my people. See, I understand the P.T.S.D, I have sexed the depression beyond my wildest dreams. See, they come to me to speak, not understanding, I'm part of the missing pure greatness that's waiting for the help. See, they're missing out on compassionate love topped with a little innocence being snatched away while you start to walk through neglect.

See, I am pleased to please my fellow people. I have been corrupted with a selfish disease that allows me to see hearts bleed. I spread my love, I have passion 'cause I drunk my soul in exchange for fool's gold. Can I ask, my people, why are we only standing for funeral services? Success is our keeper, my people, what can we do to better our situation in this life? We're not living but surviving.

So, as I walked around the hood gathering information surrounding this topic; I got many responses, but the consistent and sincerest sound I heard was LISTEN TO US...HELP US. It is coming to a point in time where we as blacks know people only desire capital gains off our down falls and from our struggles that we survive daily. This is the key to awakening ourselves because no one is going to do it for us; it's no different from the grind.

BLINDING OPPRESSION

Let this be stated. I am fully aware of this scheme the system calls government-funded agencies/programs that are supposed to help the less fortunate people. I hate to break the truth to the ones who have spread their love, compassion and caring spirit in these agency offices. Yes, I'm sorry because love and care is not as long and strong as the dollar sign in this arena. I question these people of purpose who can't seem to work with others. I question the ones who speak badly and unhappily about the next person who happens to be doing numerous and effective things with dollars that have been allotted to the community. I want to encourage you, the community, to start demanding while you're standing; don't wait until you fall. Let the time for accountability stir up before you find yourself or a loved one at the mercy of those that only see dollar signs. Protest that you are tired of this hidden betrayal that is coming to the light and the disgusting sarcasm about your unmanageable life that's disturbing their peace. Look into the history of these agencies before you expose your hearts and thoughts, investigate the ones who are holding it up. Determine whether they're a dime a dozen or a dime that is hard to come by. Check out the agency's counter partners who are buddies and a part of the "breaking bread party."

You know how it goes; they help each other up when the other one is down. Judge every pamphlet, brochure, and flyer by the community or culture that the message is sent out to. Find the element of experience in these agencies that will best suit your situation and the reasons you are there to seek help. You have the right to be placed in the hands of someone who has the compassion to help you sort through your circumstances for solutions because they too know how it feels to need a hand. You have the right to sit across from someone who will rise to the occasion to handle you with the same care that would be extended to their loved one. You have the right to not be treated like just another client but as a human being.

Something this government fails to realize is the thought of who better to work with someone who has faced a personal war than one who has also experienced the same type of war. That is if they want change. I must wonder would they allow heart surgery to be done by someone who never even sat in the room to watch it done or mastered it just by the book itself.

After seeing such propaganda in these agencies, meetings, programs and conferences etc., I tend to wonder whether these bad cops are the only ones being seen when its people who are truly lost or need help but are sold a "government dream." Has anybody stopped to question what the heck is going on here? Am I saying that everyone who walks into a facility for help can be saved? No; however, as I sit and watch my people counted as an amount and not receive the services they need from agencies that promote gleaming mission and vision statements, I'm baffled by how much time and energy is put into these uneducated so-called trainings made of policies and procedures that existed when only so much that is occurring now matters.

To the government, learn to amend, some things will remain stuck because the effort is only being pushed so far. It seems to me that these agencies are good at abusing paperwork; using names that barely come through the door, from the lack of help and their so-called success rate is anything but that. Maybe so through old documentation or reputation. I hate to see my people that want greatness and worth not getting half the respect they deserve; using my community for you to stay afloat but you refuse to redirect your thinking to give them a "chance."

Don't let me begin to rage about the way the system is abusing our youth. Coward out to laws you hate to comply with. You're teaching them to back bite as you do. And for those who sit by silently; you're also teaching them how to not stand up to injustice and stand for something worthwhile. Has it ever occurred to anyone that entering the community to effect changes may be the answer? Go observe, ask the right questions, and most importantly listen. Instead of singing the same song of "It's the higher ups, I'm just doing my job." Educate the community on how to address the government on a local and state level to stand up for the many policies and procedures that will help you to really help them. If you truly care, stop bowing down to ways you yourself barely believe in and stop pushing things to the side.

If you really care, help us fight! Have politics with greater purpose as you tell the young ones. Follow their purpose, help yourself help us, please do your best by applying productive force to help amend some things if nothing else.

Now to my people; be very CONSCIOUS of these people you open your doors up to that ask you to sign your kids up for programs. If your child has a revolving door father, why place them in a program that will produce the same results in his/her life? A program that will come promising everything and delivering nothing. A program that is here today and gone tomorrow.

Don't look for a baby sitter. Look for a place that provides a healthy community that cultivates a sense of self-worth. Let it be somewhere that is at the very least transparent about what they can actually offer and will strive to plant enough seeds into a child's life to later produce the greatness hidden within your child. Read everything, research, and ask solid questions before enrolling your child or yourself in any program.

THIS is not for all, it is for many. If the case-management fits the client described, then handle your caseload. To my people working for these agencies, stay strong. Many say we learn what not to do to comfort our pain when indeed, easier said than a pained passion. Let's just do our best to get away. Find necessary structure to establish self by all means positively.

And as for the government; do you really want these crimes to stop? Do you really want to help people gain knowledge and understanding or do you want them to slow down just enough to catch up?

I'm still waiting to figure that one out, and if you don't mind me asking, wasn't crack-cocaine eating away at homes in the urban communities just as heroin is eating at a little of all communities?

Thank you for your support. The oppression is truly over if you are blind!

BATTLE LINES

Where I live is the city of the devil inside the world of kings and queens. Why can't we see our worth? I am faced with adversity on my city corners with my friends and my kin. I have come to grasp the greatest adversity of all, which is the cycle of sin within. I was a man lost, so lonely inside.

I have grown up with the home training of a dog left outside in winter weather. I can't say accomplishments give the push, I will say it gives me the insight of an unknown book. I am shown in this world that there's nothing truly to miss. If I was a child with that missing father I couldn't say, "Man, I wish!"

I'm now wandering, but where am I going? Maybe it's just the journey I have chosen that got me tired. I'm fighting for change around change while being changed with respect enough to help the next gain. Tired, lost, in pain and wondering about my son. I'm wishing to give him this new daddy shining brighter than the unwanted dim sun. My baby doesn't know I've been crying before him at seeing myself in space and picturing my death without a bitter taste, but my son can't understand this.

I have spread hope and so much care while fighting a disease of destruction I do not fear. I am seeing many minds and insights while the truly needed and worthy is ungiven. I am regressing in my depression and one may ask so why go to such a place? You don't know what they said about me and you don't see what I see. I'm trying to mend my heart and my piece of the world, but there are cutthroats all around me. Why go to such a dark place? How about you tell me?

Well, my comfort was built in a place of hood grace. I fight for those who have no know-how or no chance. Being such a man never being created or helped to transition is a fight many want, and some don't care to understand. What I can say is I want my brothers back, better yet, forget it. Send me where they are, give me the place of peace. Why, I ask God, would you rather see me self-destruct? Haven't I sacrificed enough? Called every bluff and still I see. I was told you have something special and for this pain I can think of plenty. At the same time my mind isn't holding well for the plenty.

Free Writing By 1 Love 2 Many Struggles

COMING FOR YOU

    Some things I refuse to take seriously because I wholeheartedly believe there is a *"pure cure"* for my community. I watch my people in poverty while destroying and humiliating themselves while you sit in these high-powered chairs blowing high powered smoke. We as a community sometimes possess a low level of thinking. Our destructive mindsets have and continue to kill our own brothers, sisters, cousins and parents through ignorance of wanting a better life for ourselves. We refuse to accept that quicker is not always better.

    I personally do not believe that it is always a mental health issue; sometimes believe it or not, we might just need love. Now, let that soak in.

    How can you approach a person who has reached the great age of thirty, hear him express his experience of growing up in an environment that was contrary to what love looks like? He tells you that closest he has come to knowing this great thing called love is from the TV screen he's posted in front of or the book that holds up his prison cell floor. Interestingly enough, he has yet to experience the passion many great love novels speak of and expect him to truly comprehend love.

    We are not asking for your land, we are asking for care in many forms. We are asking to be recognized and not categorized to the lowest degree. I observe houses sitting in my community with broken windows and debris from house fires for who knows how long. Crack pipes and needles commonly lay on the ground as children pass by. Our streets are so broken and not one thought is given to the reality that the neglected potholes are tearing up the vehicles of hardworking individuals that will one day have to choose between necessary car repairs or provisions for the family. This should not be so.

    I must wonder when I drive through "other" neighborhoods how do they get these rush clean ups, why aren't their streets just as bad as the ones destroying the cars in my community? The disparities go on and on. This relationship between us and them has been built from hate, humiliation, stolen dignity, displacement, discomfort and many more unpleasant experiences and feelings. Who are the real animals in this dysfunctional realm? I ask this in silence but with a loud burst of aggression, the kind when my elders use to tell me "don't act like that in front of these people. They are already scared."

Yes, the feeling is so real, PURE and ROOTED straight from the heart. I'm a young black man just asking for some clarification about me and my other young black brothers' and sisters' struggles. Didn't our people fight hard enough? I know some of you may say yes, they did but not smart enough…. Well, I hope you see the seed in this young one coming for your destruction!

I SEE

Not hard for me to see the bullcrap people have to offer. I come to realize the seriousness of something needing to change. I can't say much for my elders these days. Is a village doing a child peace and justice? The wisdom seems to have been swept away along with the love and hearing a child scream. How are we all down and no one seems to want no one to get up? The knowledge these days from elders seem dangerous to take in. I feel the fire on every side being a young black man. Why should I have to feel such from the wisdom in my culture or so-called elders? A chain is strong as its weakest link, well I hate to see how it's being picked up. It has definitely broken and its only left to my young ones to pick up the pieces left from the broken chain, the only thing is have they been molded to reconstruct?

I hate to watch my young black brothers and sisters killing each other over nothing. I know we have nothing as young blacks, so we fight for it all. That block is our home and we're taught no love, so we get attached to the love of loyalty. That "nigga" we call our brother and sister is family, a bond no one can break.

We've out done some serious struggles together so when someone comes through and takes this bond/family from this greatness we call earth it's time to prove the trueness of this love. For we want only the abundance of such. If they tempt us, we react the only thing my loved ones taught us. We are so broken in sight from suffering from such because we don't see the mirror affect that person is us! We must understand the first thing to arm self with in this war is RESPECT and SELF. I mean deeply we must learn other forms of integrity/morals. We must become deeply rooted throw away the sane (best way to hide something from a black man is put it in a book). We must educate ourselves on many different things, no longer am I just walking in the store. I now understand the marketing strategy that's put in place and how the ignorance in my community is the big boom.

With self-development, we will no longer enter their prisons; we'll learn to understand our potential better. They know we were brought up on survival and challenge. We adapt without a doubt because we know and have seen things that breed us and not teach us. We must pick up the pieces and no longer remain a slave to the foolishness they dangle in our faces. We go crazy to spend while the ones who are against us go crazy to invest. We need to learn not only strategy and strength but humility because if one controls your emotions, they definitely alter your movements. Whether you believe or not, they will control your currency. Sacrifice is one balance that we need to properly understand, also. If not, how can we understand where we come from? Don't forget the lives that were taken to keep us marching properly!

RECOVERY

What is this system planning on doing to my people? When I say "my people" I'm not saying just blacks, I'm speaking for the unconscious and struggling. Those of us who come from chaos, who are now seeing the truth, and are attempting to give back and help wake one another up!

Again, I ask, what are they going to do with us? What is the use of having the map to freedom when the entire family is enslaved and not a one is willing to share the map? One can't give all vision and understanding, but there are many in life that are in proper spirit, who when faced with such in the right form is willing to take the love of the spirit and learn to respect such blessing. We have no true strength if we don't pursue or use what was given to us even if it was just a struggle. Let not those who heard or think they know what they are talking about do something for the mighty dollar, but let us, the ones who have faced these tragedies, speak up, give out and don't hold back. Just because we recover doesn't mean there are not things still out there that needs to be uncovered with pure rooted greatness!

WHERE I COME FROM

I came from a toxic family, school system, and environment /community. My value system was shaped by my sight, my seeing and hearing all that was around me. I was raised in the streets, slums, ghetto, hood; whatever name fits the broken mindset. Poverty is the word that plays most in politics, on a more proper occasion. I grew up watching my parents have their drunken fights, hearing their abusive language and card parties like many others around my way.

In my family, I watched true money being made and legends being created (royal street respect). I've seen shootings, robberies and all the drugs you could think of being pushed. I jumped in the streets doing crimes by the age of eight and they only got worse and riskier. It was the best life ever, but the worst feelings always sunk in my heart and stomach. I branched off in myself, falling in love with what I was starting to see myself as, knowing I would soon be there.

I ended up falling into many different crowds of friends who had one thing in common, the (aggression) game, which fit me right in. Soon, I touched a little drank and weed at age 12 and that wasn't the first time, just first time where I felt the feeling more enjoyable than before and kept it up. I ended up having a father who tried to commit suicide several times and a mom who to me was heartbroken more than a child could understand and was just looking for her comfort.

When I was eleven, my twelve-year-old sister was mainly there for me. By 13-14, I was living alone with a shadow that came around every now and then. On and off it stayed that way; I was alone besides in the streets. Family wise, only when in sight if in sight.

I was in love with the worse street drug, the "streets". I ended up in and out of juvenile detention center here and there for theft, loitering, menacing, rioting, stolen cars, high speed chases, robbery, burglary and the list goes on.

By the time I reached adulthood, I was sent to do over 6 years in prison for a shooting and other charges. It was like I got out here because I liked the love and needed to fend for myself. I fell in love with the true family and love of the streets. I put myself last for a blast of to just be there. My life was gone. I served 3 years in a level 2 prison and shipped to max security, which is known in some cases to execute death row prisoners, then placed in two other max housed prisons. It's like I sat in my cell and asked where did life go? Me and my walls, not a piece of true human life seem necessary here!

STEP INSIDE: CONSCIOUS

As hurt pushes the mind so strongly, its power pushes so seriously, it even brings questions of hold on to the physical; valuable in ways this pain can soar, adapting furiously to the point I-ness in consciousness can't collapse, it only can soar. Feral in thought because fickle is the environment we as in "I" the body and the mind stands, inattentive to self "not if I was blind"; one is so strongly conscious within isolation to this blizzard, I'm even more of a I-man. I speak so confident inside concentration is the heart, combination is the mind, fascinated by calculating the adventure of this hurt and numb to the physical pain not naïve, so one has to truly be sapient of self to override this pain.

Actual Journal Entry in Solitary Confinement at North Central Correctional Facility
2010

TRUE-MAN

One is defined by one's own actions. Ignorance is admirable to the fools plus knowledge is energy in the mental and heart of a *True-Man:* One who is *Responsible* for their actions. Pride is the tool of a child and in a fool, insecurities run deep, when you've only went so deep to search in self. In a conscious life we grasp onto edifying values and realize and approach our challenges instead of run from them. I strive because I believe my demeanor will speak volumes: Frustration gives a fool "cravenly" courage to abandon true thoughts. God speaks high in one's heart; it's the true-remedy to gain self. Divorcing our self from it makes us suffer without being conscious of "I," we'll tend to feel it's "meaning" our actions are "sapient." I am glad I've learned to retreat in positive resources, the wealth of self, knowledge, and wise character. It's hard in life when we walk around so obtuse; our only opportunity is to be fickle to the whispers of true-self!

1love 2many Struggles

Free Writing By .... Grinell Tyson Jr. Lucasville 2012

LISTEN UP! ANOTHER GUN

    Well, I finally had my sight plugged. I am not tired of the system; I'm tired of the people in it. They say we are one, we will help you if you want different.... So on and so on, it's a bunch of bull if you ask me! I have a strong dislike for these people, I am beyond tired and I refuse to stress myself out because of what everyone wants besides truly coming together. I will reach for my greatness and gather as much greatness as I can. I will pursue and do, but I only can do so much. Still, I will fight tooth and knife through day and night.... straight jungle. Even if I fall, my heart will remain standing! But not just to say I was that man because this is for my people!

Exiting a Social Service Agency
2015

RESPECT & UNDERSTAND

Doing all you can to understand these individual's mindset without first respecting them. This is what these agencies, grant writers, program directors, and local officials are doing wrong. Let's ask this question; would you allow someone in your home to move your furniture around because they feel or even know it would look better over here or there or healthier towards the wall? When we step into someone's culture no matter inherited or created as the days go, we must find every-non-judgment bone in our body to take in these (humans) greatness. From the smallest to the biggest of why their style of clothing is such, down to their hair and music, to the point of their comfort with the air that surrounds them. See, now we're speaking on a higher playing field.

Coming up, I heard a lot of elders say it takes a village to raise a child. Let me ask this; when did it stop being a village? From what I see and know these villages may have lost their values and know nothing about the business of integrity; many can't even mentally tend to themselves but please know there is still a village out here in this place you call society. Yes, there are many different elements to the village now days. How they are being perceived is what needs to be investigated! Comprehending the concept of a person or culture begins by respecting the instrument you're dealing with. You must break down any preconceived notions and stereotypes to see beyond the external appearance and long enough to properly assess what is needed internally. It must be a lot about non-judgment and respect when it comes to understanding culture. We may not like the screams in each other's music, we may have uneasy feelings and opinions about the walk, talk, dance, hand shake, style of clothes and many other things but we close up mentally because we have no understanding fully clear of far as the abuse, ways and use.

I-AM

I-am love, I-am pain, I-am loyalty,
I-am brave, I-am respectful, so very respected
I-am hearts break and I-am heart broken,
I-am a body with a 1000 hearts, I-am a heart hoping to pump
I-am needing.......
Chapter one of a broken mind, body, heart and soul
such wise spirit keeps these flames burning only on these cell walls,
but it's so hard knowing the character of abuse that has molded such a seed;
depression, stress, and betrayal still bleed,
while no compassion for passion is pure and seen
I-am accepted with a limit while limits play no parts
I-am lying down asleep while I have to face somebody who's drowned in loving me
Stepping on me through my sleep,
wondering if my awake is my dreaming, and my dreaming is my awake...
all while preparing me for the next blind betrayal attack

I-am in love with the insane and pleasure myself
with risk, knowing courage is the mighty person
not only true strength, but the remedy to my life's
gift;
Is it so indeed insane to be insane through the next
one's brain? Being pleased with and through the
unpleasing;
structure is coded and placed and at the end,
still only a man is there to take his place,
I-am, I- am, I- am such man!

THE PAIN OF HOOD

"HOME"

Have you ever had to sit with self and had to
REFLECT?
Have you ever experience pain you don't need a doc to
tell you it's bad for your health?
I'm speaking a pain and loneliness so deep,
You feel as you're the seed for heart break mixed with
a drop of mental health,
I always wonder what my parents thought
about this child
they put out into the world,
Then consciousness kicks in,
to place and bless the body with a solid mind to say
there's no time to think,
My whole life I been alone,
My whole life I begged for a home,
Being labeled as a child that grew up
but still lost in his first home,
I'm tired of loving,
I'm tired of caring,
I swear run to look for comfort
think I got it just to get the same scare,

Too old for this longing
but still it doesn't leave like my untrusting fear,
Always found comfort in the wrong things
guess cause' it was no direction there,
My soul shakes sometimes rushing to get home,
But still lost in these streets
with no care of that home,
I can careless who don't respect my words
for that let me know
they haven't felt my **HOME**!

"STRENGTH HOPE FAITH"

Dealing with destiny through broken love,
Replaying nothing but hope mentally,
Optimism has become my long-lost friend of friends,
While success sits in my heart,
Truth being nothing but my hug when time of rest,
Sad is my keeper when spirit is not intact,
While body sits shocked,
From reality of my days of on comings,
Playing strong to live in this game, knowing strength is oneself true PEACE,
Dying to love self for that's the remedy to walk this Queen,
While faith is bleeding out my body pure and unseen,
Honesty to my son is what really keeps the blood on run,
Letting this inner PEACE elevate me,
But tears still run wild as one sits honest with self,
Pushing towards this bright but empty future,
Still the sounds of **STRENGTH, HOPE AND FAITH**,
Plays repeatedly in the subconscious of one true self!

*This was written about someone who placed great understanding in my life. She is on the edge to fight the fight of her life.

"READY"

For entertainment of the mind, Learning survival through unwanted harsh times,
Looking for a father but settling with a gone mom had to be fine,
Destruction been my calling, Menace to society I heard a few people scream along with some judges say,
What they didn't know is my dreams hasn't always been so unwanted and ugly,
Fell in love with art and engineering was my calling, got into sports and loved it more than just some hobby,
I sat staring in the audience at the spelling B knowing my Dad would come but guess that wasn't his calling,
"Responsibility" was the word I misspelled,
Only if I was taught first hand maybe just maybe I could have got that word,
Instead sitting around grown kids was my hobby,
Playing fake sex games, acting as we're smoking cause the environment kept such reality that could only make a child curious and lonely,
Having big sis give me some of that wild rose, while big cuzz kept me and lil cuzz too exposed,

See where I grew up and not raised had no choice but to be READY,
Watching everyday being lived on the edge,
Thousands of parents with lost kids,
This is not to say as you grow, one doesn't have choices,
But being ready for the worse was our environment loud voices,
Cause crime gon' come and time gon' come,
But making it out was the choice with that smoking gun,
So, to the ones getting READY I say,
I apologize for any unwanted on comings
Cause' being READY doesn't mean to never respect self,
Not to take care of the kids you create
Or the next dollar is a block away,
But to just weed out the loud noises
Because then you would be READY to pave the way,
That no one in these environments is willing to teach us today!!!

"BEAUTIFUL TRAUMA"

She loved me and took me in,
Played me but raised me like I was her closest kin,
We were so close I felt and heard her heart beat...
A sound that was O so sweet,
She bled in my arms many of nights,
She used to tell me....
one more night of fighting off these bad guys
We'll be alright,
Tighter than the closest of friends but still trauma she
placed from beginning to end,
I used to cry when she called,
Lonelier than some but loved all over,
She gave me a blanket quite beautiful it was,
Many nights I smelled it just to remember her hug,
Her best friend was mines too,
She robbed us both that night,
But that's what a friend does
cause if not it wouldn't be right,
Living a life most would call trif,
Only way she knew to live... so why judge her right?
Father took advantage so why not the hood right,
She was only promiscuous,

Lease that's what the voices say,
Momma was dead wrong to leave such young lady left alone,
Watching the cuts on her wrisk grow,
Seeing that beauty cry through a boarded-up window,
Wondering where she is today,
Those hunting images might say,
Well she is successful in and out,
So now what trauma have to say,
.... Dang right that beautiful soul made a choice to make a way,
And that's because she used trauma as her **MIGHT**!!!!

*This is just some insight from growing up around young women in the community where I grew up. Witnessing so many lost and hurt young Queens. Having young girlfriends smiling outside but scared to go home. Being hurt in so many ways by the men in and near their life. Leaving them not knowing how to handle or trust much anymore; But also looking for comfort in so many wrong ways. This is for the ones who stories still haven't been told today and all those young women who turned their pain into their power!

"REALITY"

Is reality this selfish, this unkind,
How well can one live in an ocean of unseen love,
How pure can one be in a city of sin?
How true should I be even though they sometimes give,
I scream this very loudly... **Is there truly a friend?**
Greatly spoken for one who doesn't even believe in such,
My take is you must give what you can get,
But wouldn't that be a waste of value,
Replace with the lack of settlement,
I pick wisely when it's time to give
cause my reality, ...
is a life with buried kids
Yes! Dead before they even arrive on this thing some call earth,
I like the word "planet" better cause nothing exists,
Just a false reality that keeps on giving!

Free Writing By 1 Love 2 Many Struggles
Sincerely Grinell Tyson Jr.

"THOUGHTS AND PRAYERS"

Asking questions to be saved, while relaxing at young friends' graves,
Character is the seed of life,
But with no understanding prayers can never bless the body right,
Screaming hate inside,
Looking for family but being left outside,
Being the bud of a joke just for on lookers to get by,
Watching death play its role right outside,
Got a step but no door… but that's the best way to southside,
Looking for closeness in a field full of knives,
"That could never be alright,"
Tired of wearing this smiling hateful face,
Relaxing in thought wanting prayer to be my faith,
Looking for something higher to help the mind, body and soul get to a better place,
Knowing my home is my home so I'll make due to just be okay!

"TIME IS SUICIDE"

Being sincere in this silence,
Knowing how my greatness shines,
Conscious of my worth,
So I refuse to waste this P.E.A.C.E,
A weapon to who wants to hold me...Cause that's the only way I shall and will share this P.E.A.C.E,
See my parents taught me well from a distance,
So that in itself always allowed me to know what to give,
Just as well as what I was missing,
I stand to see greatness in all who I encounter,
Even when greatness is far seen from the beholder's Eye/I
In life time is your best friend.... so party up!
But be very aware of yo' give,
One has to understand that the gift of time is to preserve their present,
Cause without pure true rooted understanding you're playing a dead man's game,
And that game gets one no further than a grave of regrets,
Yaw better hear this man speak,

Because if you knew about his time, you would pick yours up and GRIND!!!

*(P.E.A.C.E) I use many different acronyms for the word peace. In this writing for me it just means positive energy. Eye-Is the visual that one can see through sight with no forced effort. I-means your mental, when you have breathed in information and have become rooted to the core with oneself.

"UNKNOWN"

I got that feel, that seems a bit too real too unreal,
I'm back sitting with these worried visions,
Hoping my life's purpose isn't one of a killing,
Sitting with this evilness on my shoulders,
Watching as the gates open,
But being pulled away like my lost faith, when duty is to only be punished,
It's time to reach out to ask is my time coming,
Feeling this unknown kill in my stomach like deaths coming,
Praying that my son and unborn child get to see daddy rumble,
Still I feel success is in my sky,
So I look up with hopes of all kind,
Praying retiring from this earth with unwanted sins isn't my last calling,
Something shaking my body without a break,
Hoping it's just a trick to keep the mental on play,
No gaming for me right now, Cause life's unknown is seeming as my fate,
What's a man without a destiny...hope it's not on my life's plate,

Wonder if they hear me crying inside,
Knowing that my outside is a wish I rather not decide at this time,
I guess for right now, I'll sit sickly with this unknown worried fate!!!

"I DON'T KNOW"

Hurt is standing near, but growth is the tool that cares,
But pain overrides sometimes to explain its loving care,
While sleeping,
confused thoughts touch my body with the worst swears...To My God that is,
Knowing fear is just false appearance...the mind plays to be real,
My only weapon is change ...so I know its time to give,
Happiness I need, but being lost in sadness is my friend,
Focus is my eye, So that's the only strength that gives,
Being a better person is where my spirit lives,
Understanding myself...Just knowing myself,
Being a better mother is where I live,
Selfishness been my down fall so now selfless shall live,

So I will now push to only love my self unconditionally, Because I know that's where **I DON'T KNOW** truly lives...!!!

*The above was about someone who sat and expressed while I typed. Just hope she now knows Her "don't know".

"I WANT"

Today I Just want my dad to pick up the phone,
Today I just want momma to say daddies coming home,
Today I wish for daddy not to lie,
Today I wish just to trade another kid places just to see how a dad is cause can't say I ever been to such place,
Too young to be dealing with this so big of a pain,
Didn't ask to be alive so why can he decide not being here would be alright,
Hate that my dad would choose his pleasure of life over the pleasure of having a child,
Wanting him to play catch or give a hug shouldn't be too much,
He always lies too but acts like he's a man,
I was told a man has his word but guess I'm just too young to understand,
Why name me after you,
Was it just to say you have and can,
I hope when he comes to see he lost out, that he'll still be proud to know not him, but my momma made me one great man!!!

*I experienced being in the presence of another man's child for the first time.
It was a blessing and a lesson.

STRUGGLE

All love to the ones who show this struggle love,
thanks for I've fell too far,
I smile for (I) realize the fall,
I carry with worry to show my realization,
afraid is far gone,
for I've seen the worst of struggle,
my love is like stone to protect what I've created,
I build with the strength I was once weakened from,
I know the beauty of life, and will only treat myself
as a king, knowledge has built a machine of no return,
love has showed me the foolishness I thought was
love
my sadness laughs to keep the strength of happiness
to be back with the ones who stuck it out
with this harsh,
heart broke, tearful
Struggle!

UNMANAGEABLE

VICE- Immoral or wicked behavior. How does one understand and get ahold of such?

Coming up in an environment that taught you the training of an animal in the wild. I sit lost at times running to the things that break character or hold one back from true self. Dealing with the habits of an unshaped child. Lost with a mentality not many understand or just ready to prejudge. Why does the young man run to the bottle as a baby who hunger pain can't last any longer? Why does aggression take over his being as it's the perfect remedy to get him through whatever is currently going on. Why does self-destructing capture his soul like that grown up music to the old folks. How does one learn to understand management of well-being and value, when no one have led him to the water of wealth? I'm lost on this path at times just from unmanageability. Finding out my handle is a vice ready to give worse and no good. I want understanding but a lost child who never found a lead leaves such body empty with pain. I bleed nails and bullets and broken glass becomes the tears once they have met the ground. Really just a man untaught and never trained by a father and seek most times the things a mother brings (nurturing). My painful emotions over ride me sometimes but not with the handle of a true man. I do not want to leave this earth misunderstood, looking like a father's baby curse because he chose not to wear a condom or use his brain but instead ran because he couldn't deal with reality and be a true man. Not understanding where the issues will lead that young boy who has not been led. I'm lost for the better sometimes; lease I feel when trying not to witness my behavior or the reality I bring in and to my life sometimes. I know that life is not filled with pain and destruction is not the great way. Just this program that shaped the unparented left child sometimes leave him in the unhealthy vice way. How to un-train such beast that has found his only way to feast just from being a baby beast. He never had a rattle he had a gun. He never had a home only the slums. He never witnessed true leadership only project homes. So where does this lead this vice filled child? I pray in a heaven where everything isn't the same as what he always had to numb from.

"1 STORY"

As stories are great to read,
but this I'm living,
Only a story of the best worst novel
How to see when hooked in bar clouds, how to feel my face when the man in the mirror is a mistake replaced
How do I erase this novel of worst?
Why so young and heart cursed?
Why should and do I hate the love
not many people show me,
My best learning is within me,
I choked on my own blood to help people,
but in my normal life I'm used to them leaving me,
how....? Wow...! this hurts when it hits the fan,
But blow you far away
Because you never believe your own face had and can....

A BEAUTIFUL PAIN

See I got this pain that's so fine she's beyond a dime,
she got me here hurting, she shows me no respect,
If I were her child, the phrase would be "neglect"
all I want is her love, its bad when they say
"man is the strong one"
but yet my sexy pain, she breaks me down...
boy am I in trouble searching for love,
I should've known better...
"strap up, protection, a glove ...."
but the heart doesn't seem to work that way...
plus, my pain man, she just got that power,
that kind that you find you ain't know was your thang,
she keeps me smiling in and out,
I gave up my soul in trade for love,
she seems to still not give a care....
We ate and laughed yesterday.... yup she took me out,
ain't that something
only thing like always, she got on that phone,
something told me once again I was being left out
...tuh,
there she goes, That's my pain!

"A PRAY FOR LOVE"

I pray for love
I pray for love,
Please give me one to hug
I pray for love
I pray for love,
Please give me one to hold
I pray for love
I pray for love,
Please forget the sins I did and give me that question I have all the answers to
I pray for love
I pray for love,
When will my day come where I can just touch
I pray for love
I pray for love,
Now I'll get off my knees and hope you'll accept My Lord please!

"FOR PRAYERS OF LOVE" 2

From my heart.... I love you
From my soul....
I'm blessed to have a woman as you,
With your unconditional love on my side,
Exquisite as you are, there's no denying my "in love" with you
For shattered tears and extreme blood rushing,
I pray with a rushing love disease with all faith,
And knowing you're praying of hoping our day of togetherness will come....
Knowing the wealth of your seriousness,
the promise of our love will drown
But 'till that day,
My wife....
I'll take love from your prayers...
To our overwhelming caring,
Inordinate desire of lust for our love......
Crash with "in love" ....
And a journey into new life!

"Sister In Mind"

For the love of sis
For the love of sis,
I wish you great days
For the love of sis
I'm glad to know and say you're sis everyday
For the love of sis
For the love of sis,
Please stand tall for me while I have these worst days
For the love of sis
"Precious Marie Tyson"
I'll pray for today and ask the Lord to forgive me as my loving sister say,"
And hold my hand as promised past my due date
So, Lord bless Precious and forgive me for my bad days

*My sis wrote me while I was incarcerated and gave me some kind words and told me to pray. So I wrote this in dedication to my sister; what she didn't know, I was going through my worst.

"Deep seeking of destiny"

I been calling on you
I been calling on you,
I've searched everywhere
I went from momma house to grandma house,
And now I'm back downstairs
I don't know if you're a plan or a goal
When I looked' you wasn't there
Maybe you're a prayer
Maybe a little faith
Maybe you're God , just with a different face
I'm not sure if it's my time
Or I'm not sure if I should wait
I'm answering questions without questions
So that leaves me with weary fate
As I sit down and think to myself
Somethin' in my heart tells me it gotta be a better place
But the sin on my skin
Is burning me as if I was already sitting in the devil's face
Internally I want greatness and I know greatness
But externally, greatest seem the farthest from my sight
Even though I know it's my third eye

But it's hard to see when the scares and the tears are overwhelming me
See I fear nothing, but I respect all
I know god is good in everyone's heart
But it seems as for some reason I just hold on to the fall
As one of those dreams people speak of
And the next day can't recall
See I know my fate is coming
And understand that I create my own circumstance
So I know the might is in my thought process
Cause that's where the almighty lay his hands
See what I'm searching for
Is the position to be a better man
Looking for a friend within me
But only coming up with the enemy within me
See I know my soul is cold and broken as could be....
but still I ask for this blessing that everyone say they see.

"ONE PLACES INTRANSIGENT THROUGH THE PERCEPTION OF IGNORANCE"

We root character through the reflection of surrounding and one's habit repeated action, ignorance is there for place, and leaves so much replacement for gain,
conscious staying one's own fool and the world hated tool, intransigent could only be such genius tool, desiring the determination for manifestation must be sagaciously pure
rooted to pain the pleasure of the habit of self-inflicted abuse,
keen in common sense will find its un-ruled but blindly abuse, surrounding the self with such reflection is the mirror affect

to stand the pain of proper self-purpose brain attack!

*Sometimes one must learn to step outside their normal abusive pattern of thinking. Even if it hurts to shut up. (Never stop being a student).

"PLEASE JUST STOP"

My heart's pleading.... bathed in pain,
I've been shedding tears again,
only this time my switch doesn't work,
so much hurt in one heart,
can't understand why it still works,
I've been hoping for a blessing, but that must not be
in my fate, when I'm sleep, it's as I'm being cut by
sharp razors all over my body,
as I look on... the only pain I feel,
is my pleading heart, *"bathed in pain"!*

"UNDERSTAND"

I understand now,
I'm myself kill
I understand now,
I'm not lonely here
I understand now,
I've been learning through and taught
I understand now,
I can control these thoughts
I understand now,
I have lesser fear that's even with faith
I understand now,
That I am not the only one hurting here!
"I love who blessed me with life",
I hate who made me live it
I pray for day and night,
"I'm not proud to understand this living"

"WHY HE HUG DEEM STREETS"

I been slummen' since I was 6 years old,
watchin' the dope man pumpin, playin' in the storm,
hearin' nothin' but loud thunder in my tracks,
I was seen when I was curve ball hustlen',
unknown to self createn' ma mind fo' thuggin',
ghetto love for Christmas I was used to unwrapped presents,
spendin' birthdays as one, two, three,
then they became a nigga curse days,
cause the cake never showed up
the only lights on,
were the streets,
I remember not seeing my peeps as a youngin'
ready for the tuck-in so I can go to sleep,
canned goods child, sugar bread wild,
first of the month I was smilin' out loud,
roaches and rats, pants and shirts for school,
it went to the habits of the house,
like our food for the mouse,
see I got plenty hugs 'cause I knew plenty thugs

dats why when it came to them streets... I was ready to hug!

A Good Man

She said, "Break it down."
I asked, "Is that so, okay?
Why am I a good man? Cause I can please you baby?
I mean inside and out my first lesson of please baby
I'm a man, so yes its care and show respect."
I understand the pictures that's drained in my woman's heart, I can also cater and go out my way , I'm not a boy so my pride and shame has no role in the play, I will not play with mine from front or behind, I can kiss my woman's body til' it shakes and this is far more pleasurable than the words I lay, I can comfort her with my love and my strength,
my woman is my passion so what that mean is nothing or no one else gets any of my action, see I'm down for riding for mines, where I'm from bluntly said, dying for mine!
I rub my woman's feet and kiss them above or under the sheets, I massage her back, I kiss her tears, I shed some to show she has a true man here!
See baby, my love doesn't stop, so no need for a ruler, cause the heart I got, it's unmeasurable!
I may can't give all the millions and material things......
to a true woman, baby I can love,

like I'm the true seed, if it was a plant or creator if it was a drug, I know how to trust, guide, believe, and touch her soul with patience, kiss her thoughts with less worries,
I can look in my woman eyes and be a man and not lie to her, see baby I can love, only thing is....
Only a real woman can get mines...
I'm not even gone tease no woman,
because I'm looking for commitment and I need all seriousness.....
So yeah I am a man, and I can love but I need me a woman.... You hear? A woman baby, who can understand and respect true love..... from a good man

"WISE TO KNOW"

Wise to know now that I know better I'll do better,
make it lifelong, positive and properly structured....
I know confidence must always be in the "I"
with first rated determination,
which I'll keep heavy inside and out
I will live up to my fullest potential,
I will use everything inside that I've learned from the external,
For I do understand the necessary,
To cherish my moments in this life that I have been given,
now I close my eyes to pray and say....
"Thank you, God,
for storing me with firm understanding and
giving me such an amazing understanding of
"Consciousness",
Amen!"

"A BOY'S ISSUES"

See I'm living proof that the heart ain't bullet proof,
And if the soul made of gold
it's got to be fool's gold'
Thorough bread in a diaper, coming up rough,
You would think I was born with a sniper,
The way I'm ready to bust,
see before I was a customer to the streets,
they were a customer to me,
I cried blood as a kid,
Seen my first slugs,
which means seen my first body as a kid,
I was welcome to a life with all guns,
but was given a knife,
I cried some nights,
Just knowing I was on my way to die unwanted them nights,
Always wanted a dad,
but couldn't keep em' around,
I guess he was too ashamed of the pad,
Lease I played it to be,
Seeing Momma couldn't teach me the 'G',

'Cause the only code she knew was broken and through,
Which if you ask me...
I could have been used as the glue,
I can't tell who was smarter 'cause I gave plenty clues,
Which once again made me the fool,
without once again a tool,
which that means only thing in my disposal,
Was no school,
but my hustle was left alone to get food,
Now my only tears at night was my sweats,
But who can complain with a nice black hoodie
for tissue to match,
Which held up well for a young nigga with grown man issues,
Macken and relaxing with them streets,
It pushes strength through my veins,
Push the blood so smooth
how couldn't that heartbeat,
especially in a boy who's soon to be a man beast!

"BELIEVE ME"

O how my blood rush,
O God why can't I stop this great pain,
O evil give me burning love,
O I need help just to maintain,
I can't believe I sell kills and save goods,
What will happen from these never look backs,
Who will treat my cold heart?
Why should I be the damned one when It's only half my part,
Now grown and lost to start,
Telling people, it's half me,
I know will only foolish me,
But how will I do it,
I guess continue to bleed out tears to die off half of me!

"CONQUER MAN CONQUER BEAST"

Betrayal in a beast of a man,
See through his soul and find your eye to be stolen,
Lost he is,
pushin' strength in his mind that only his heart can give,
Learning what love got him,
Wishing for a casket for the so-called love cry can be over with,
He feasts on old souls,
His space is only freezing to the cold,
He was sold as a child,
And layaway as a man,
His only loyalty is to self,
which is to always stand,
He breaths freedom when he sleeps,
when he's woke he's blinded with the freedom of self,
Which is only the peace within the beast,
to always know you're still loyal to self!

"DRUNK MIND"

It hurts inside... so I strike to ride
feelin' this emotion,
Mind tellin' the brain,
"I need more of this potion"
As I ignore this other side,
not carin',
Cause' I love this ride as it numbs my body
from the out 2 the inside,
Mesmerized so never care 2 die,
Feel more than just heaven as I build it myself,
Ready to commit sins like it's good for my health,
Cause' the mind so confused... Can't help myself,
As I beat up my body like I don't know myself
So confused to me...
Just me knowing anything...
everything is helpin' me destroy myself,
So I need to,
but ain't gon' let myself be,
So people don't destroy yourself...
Be more to yourself,
Cause' no matter what,
it's more to you plus better for yo' self!

*I can remember writing this lost in thought at the age of 15 years old. All I knew was this isn't what I should be doing. And truly was beginning to feel I'm soon to grow up and be just like him if I make it. Sitting in a youth treatment facility, fully getting my mental and emotional state examined by staff and self! All I wanted to do was get back home to my kid grown up life and have one of pops beers, a shot of that brandy (he keeps under the sink) and a cigarette to relax it with. Even knowing in my heart, it was something more I was looking for....

"A DRY WHY"
(HALF/HALF)

A soul of a man
But only feeds as a blind boy,
Watery eyes... But only cry when unflooded
And still too strong for itself,
How does a heart bleed and still survive?
Why only the boy sees his hunger and pain?
while bystanders stare....
Why open up when everything seems too close?
Why do I cry, but my face stays dry?...
Why when I get help, it overwhelms me?
false beliefs make me push it to the side....
Why am I only troubled with God?
When the people who know me know why life's worth living?
Why does this animal within my vein refuse great understanding and humble direction injection?
Why do I wear a hoodie when I fit all clothes?
Why do I have bad visions that can help people kill themselves?

Why do I hear things that destroys what you stand for...?
plus, your health?
Why do I write this, and tears fall down my body and they're unseen but felt?
Why should I hate who I have become, when become has taught me so much?
Why love nothing good when good answers any questions you have?
When my eyes hurt, can that count for crying?
When I love pain and envy dying, sinning,
breaking into things that are not mine,
taking what's not mine,
Taking what's not good for the body......
Am I cold-hearted?
But I love when I can buy my family things,
Love playing with my nieces and nephews,
Love helping people when they are down,
Never would I walk pass a hungry man ...,
Never would I enjoy killing a man...,
Never would I put harm in any kids or elders' way...
Does that give me an unstable heart and mind?
Or just at times I'm kind-hearted?
I know that life is not a game,
from great friends to good family,
a lovely p.o. taught me that sane...

So why, why I asked....
Why does all the young boy's actions diagnose him insane?
When he loves life like coming out the womb
But hates life like a man that can't help bleeding and knows there's an end.
Why, because of structure?
Or all hate mixing with good and evil,
If you understand because some acts are good
But the wrong thing gives you that act
so it soon melts to bad,
So, my humble I have not found,
my tears
they still refuse to bring around my heart,
I still remain to suffocate the good,
The soul still feeds to evil
now the opinion of others will probably be asking,
And now my "whys"
can't stop me from asking...
All I know is a torn child,
one eye blind, half heart bleeding,
Other side filled with rocks,
souls that eat everything
even its own self
A family without a good feed of health,
Good people that lost and wasted help,

But I know it...
Shut up!
you should have used it,
Sorry that's the other side,
And I found out if you run from both soon...
You'll chase **YOU** down!
So, what I'll do,
I'll just sit down to make a move,
"Now please,
grab a bag and bucket so you can pick up these tears"
And I'm not helping.... that's what got us here!!

*This was written in 2008 for my loving grandmother Freddie May Hines. I Love you and miss you Grandma! I was sitting in my cell first few days in receiving, waiting to get transferred to my parent institution (prison). When I was younger I started having these issues while doing time, at least I placed in my mind to be. They were about my grandmother and the way she left this earth. Which now as an adult had sent me back to my mental to revisit something. I love you Grandma and I wish I knew more how to express it back then

"EMOTIONS"

Not only one should know life,
One should understand,
create to know the place you soon to land,
Think slow move quick,
Understanding hurt is far gone,
Like being calm when the body feels shocked emotions,
Love is a place I love to go,
Hate is a place I love to go,
Emotions are serious for the minds that know,
As that push only so far
it stops it's go,
for need of no emotions will flow,
I ask whoever in tune with such shocking heart break and aching emotions to please stand...

"EYE 2 C"

Life is yours when you don't want it to be,
So, what about when you do?
Have you ever felt that "eye",
that (I) that can't see...?
Have you had things and goals that you feel can never be,
But knowing it's you in that "eye",
That (I) that can't see
that word that can't pronounce its own spelling,
Life that want to live,
Give to give when you should give 2 give you,
But purchase everything 2 everything to get right,
But stuck at that first night...
Don't know why cause' the truth is...
You're so smart to everyone else but "you"...
But you're there again,
The "eye", (I) that can't see...
So, to solve the problem you do all 2 be more than can be!

*I was 15 years old when I wrote this. Hurt, lost and all over the place. Living a life, no child should ever have to go through. Remember not knowing how to spell or read...but had so much pain I just wanted to let it out in some way. It was just so hard to see not only where I was standing, but who I was or even what I wanted to be. What's interesting is I never knew why I was writing my eye like that or like (I).

"EYE OF MY GHETTO"

I take a trip only the mind can see,
unfit parents,
Kids with kids,
Loud screams wit shots stoppin' em,
Hurt eyes filled only again with a young angel's
ghetto cries, Churches open but only to walkin' fire,
obtuse niggas claiming the white man's land
knowing uncle Sam don't rent to own,
I see open cases,
Wit open caskets,
wit no faces,
Ready for a second chance the no faces say,
but fate aint taking it,
Bottles of sin I see labeled as gin,
Beggin' and prayen' to me,
Now I'm faced with a rag,
how it's tied to my face,
Only the gun in my hand had to rob that place,
"Who killed my baby"
the melted tears on grandma face screams,
Still a mind so strong to hold the insane,
They the people spit out to say poverty,

As Haiti ain't in their back yards,
cause hurricanes exist every day in my ghetto,
So, hold the jail bars
and ask questions to see where I "G",
Then maybe the second chance you hold for me,
may only just hold me
far as this mind,
! MY GHETTO STRUGGLE BEG TO SEE!

"I CAN'T"

The love of you keeps me strong,
without you I can't go on,
I need your faith and hope
cause'
what you don't know,
You're my best support
so I'll ask of you,
Please baby hold on...
You to me is my love song,
So, without you I'll ask baby how do I go on!

"I'M LORD"

Only thing hurt is unhurt
Only heart broke is outside soul,
So, the real fo' the mind...
what lames it kill with no time
Respect to tell lookout is in to real,
So, forget soul/mind,
The heart loses its gold
shattered to glitter
made on polish,
Slip and fall... it only gives knowledge
So, means of matter reverse only love of chatter,
Kill the unsolved and that's half the problem...
Yo' words...yo' bond...,
It's fo' who leave... who love rocks...
But fo' who wants back...
Promise to God won't handle ma' facts
Cause' forget what it is ...
Soon to be... was my point,
For these is a drop of my heaven...
And now where to pray is the lord of me,
And messing over the blessing...is this lord's heaven
So, come to me and pray...

your mind can have it, only so lies of gave
you can have,
We will meet personally...
And here's the key to give only to personally... be real!

Free Writing By 1 Love 2 Many Struggles

Sincerely Grinell Tyson Jr.

*I remember sitting with my ego broken and pride all over the place. Not knowing how to calm my rage at the time. They say reality hurt and that I found out that day in 2008. Sitting in receiving getting ready to head to the prison I would be housed at for the next 6 years of my life.

"FATE"

As the heart rain,
And my pain has no umbrella,
And for real sight is unseen, For the racing anger muscles press to kill,
Life as freedom as a man is more than unreal,
Tagged as animals and numbered as deaths,
Wishing with praying hands of love, But without a guess,
Crease for visiting for the mind to impress,
Hoping for Hi's but fate is set,
So, in the pain of this storm I ask for rest,
But wet eyes won't close for the broken umbrella I stole!

*The broken umbrella is karma, you reap what you sow! What you put into this life understand it will soon stand in front of you.

"LOST #1"

How can one stand to fight for nothing?
How does one live and have understanding of nothing,
What if today is tomorrow,
How slow I've caught on,
When things come to light hopefully they'll stay on,
For life runs out to who begs for alone,
Stand I have,
But the promise remains to say how long,
Thinking and thought,
Had and brought,
Still I stand where I began my start,
Loving all I am praying before I rise to stand,
I asked to hold on to find/know,
Only where I fought for nothing I understand!

"NEVER STOP"

I never asked for this life... it believed in me
I never wanted to hurt... it just was raised with me,
I was never over spoken... I wasn't even talked to as a seed
I never got cut... I just felt and seen me bleed,
I was never a follower... just fell in the scene
I always knew and loved me... just needed some green,
I always had family... just the hugs weren't guaranteed
I always loved school... but the walk, it hugged me,
Even I like math and science... so maybe that's what kept me trying,
But if I say why live this life... when life don' lived me!
I'll stop to chance this mind in me...
So, push the pusher for I've created "G"!

1 Love 2 Many Struggles
Sincerely Grinell Tyson Jr.

"ONLY YOU CAN"

Amen to this young man for reaching ages he never thought of,
Don't bless this young man for he still refuses to stand,
Keep him with alone,
some for what he feels important,
Don't watch him and don't laugh as he still will run,
Give him treatment for his foolishness
while he is scared to grab another strong hand,
Pray to hell him
for you do not understand this foolish child of a man,
Why do you understand the wrong of him I ask?
But see no right when it's there,
Now the splash of true eyes,
But who will help open them,
Only you can young man!

"SEEK IN SELF"

No matter the views someone else seek to be you,
True as one as myself I would say, one is only strong as their mind,
Education empowers you to seek beyond one's physical eye,
Thinking pushes your thought, which can push your understanding and create one with better action,
Ignorance drowns fools to settle with being dumbfounded of themselves,
Use what's at your disposal...
I was taught to be conscious of who you are, stay beyond one's eye,
And within self as in (I),
You only gain from the temple when you penetrate one's 3rd eye,
beyond which some humans will never reach,
to know is also showing and dominating this process,
you will and can only reap what you sow,
So, beware of the rain or prodigy of knowledge that will consciously grow!

*Being conscious one must be willing to open their mental up. To be penetrated by wisdom and understanding far greater than their own. Stepping outside yourself and becoming aware to all things in existence. Then you have finally opened your 3rd (I). Then and only then, you'll soon become rooted with one of life's greatest and humble gifts wisdom and understanding.

"SILENCE IN THE CELL"

"Silence"... breathing is heard,
Fire is seen... A man in a cell I'm sicken' to see,
As the wind blow, I watch with no window,
I catch myself speakin' to a man only seen as brick,
I'm waiting for love like a cover in the cold,
Shivers turn to bitter... sitting on steel to flush my body out,
Taking showers in these walls where more than any man would ask to stand,
Missing kids voices the joy they bring,
Back to my thoughts slamming doors has been chilling in the mind,
Must be from the thoughts of a man not only faced with un-loyal family,
But his survival got him prison time,
Grinding was only cool when the cash was being used,
no tools left in this mind's disposal just walls to do,
While forced with no heat,
Men praying more less begging for the same things I wished to eat,

Walls been froze but the cell on fire,
Seems to me LC34 should've been state law,
As shut down and retired,
Can only think who else these walls have sunk,
The only light witnessed is the slot from mail,
If and whenever it comes in,
And no man has witnessed seeing that light,
So, when darkness seeks many,
I shall only let them seek my "silence"!

1 Love 2 Many Struggles

Sincerely Grinell Tyson Jr.

"TAKING HER LOVE"

Her heart cries out to me trying to get me to see,
that only she loves me and understands me,
Which is the only thing her mind and heart has sum up is only she can complete me,
She's crying in silence out loud,
She seems to be pushing cold on her warm,
She has death in her face that put this place in her eyes,
That will see through my heart,
She has only one emotion and it's loving me,
She'll have me anyway I direct her,
She cries blood to show me the power of her love,
She wants only her to push comfort on me even if it's just a hug,
All this love I've been faced with for only my eyes, heart, and mind can see...
And with all honesty my love is so scared,
It's only problems I can't get it to quit rushin' to this woman's love,
Who if betrayal to her comes,
Death has no fear!

"THANK YOU FAMILY"

For all who want a blessing...
Fall to one knee and say Amen,
For all who know me wish I will for the power of can,
Give me the warm heart cause cold will only push your hands,
Believe I love you family and want better for this hopeless boy of a man,
I'll take all I have, to give me what I don't have,
And that's only half the crisis at hand,
I thank you all for dropping to one knee to give me warm praying love...and in heart really do understand,
And I forgive all who said, cause' I will make better of this man!

"THE GREATEST CARE"

My great love that I hardly show,
It's truly there if your heart feels of any whys of know,
I'm glad fo' knowing I have the greatest wish of my day,
I wouldn't want more if you said okay,
I dream of nothing less because the you... you give will more than less brighten my darkened day,
I was blessed without a prayer as an angel looked over me,
I have understandings that only you can see,
I have you for direction, and now or never see any exits,
Everything we have I cherish,
The feeling of my heart feels like every second is a poor kid's wanted Christmas,
I ask questions inside and have millions of I knows,
I can't believe! I feel great!
Are answers that show for thinking of you my huge great care,
I love you and welcome you,
Even more to know that my love for you sure

and truly always will be there....
My love!

"TILL I DIE"

Anything I can have... I wouldn't pass you for it,
Anything I ever felt... you would be the most best part of it,
Hold on to your feel, Cause' it can be the last experience of it....
Why let things go when the first was just a test for it,
Why give up on me when now I'm happy for it,
Why not look at my sorry and see I'm sad over you...
What's wrong with me seeing now?
Does that count for being found, better than lost?
Give me the chances you gave...
And I promise I'll show you to the day of my grave!

"TOO MANY CHANCES"

Why does my heart cry and I complain to no one in the sky?
Why do I feel faith but an evil soul overrides?
Why am I so grown and in the front so young?
Why do I hate myself for not crying, but try every night and day?
Why is there a sparkle in my eye but it never shines?
Now the crying begins but only blood falls the cry now...
I sit dry body and wonder why the poor old young heart won't quit beating,
Yes! Now I feel the burning coming back from this unbloodied body killing....
"No Lord, Please not yet, the family... wait I'll try...."
" But son it's too late" ... No, I can cry please lord,
I try to have faith... it's not my fault
The "devil" has my heart in an angry place!
"Please lay down son...Cross your arms...
Tell your family goodbye cause' you'll burn and cry,
"Precious! Stephanie! Mom! Dad! Mama! Myja! Malachi! Samaria, Kenyoda, Toya!"
"Please help! They tried but.... But...

"No Buts! Let that evil heart learn to fry!"

"UNIQUE"

Her mind needs kisses,
While her heart needs love,
Her smarts are **"Unique"** just as the name,
The heart... it inspires my brain,
The path she leads has pushed haters to not understand,
A woman she is!
A young lady she leads,
The love I have for her only for a wife indeed,
The moments I have with her once upon a time were only seen as dreams,
The softness of her lips makes me promise to please her,
And love her body till' it screams to her,
But more and more I'll dream for us as this time more than just heal us,
I'll do no more than give respect to us,
For the love and trust we stand for as us,
"I love you Bae"...

"WHY THIS"

I ask myself many questions...
Why was I not taught much better?
Why was I seeing drunken parties?
Why was I seeing parents fighting?
Why was I forced to choose?
Why was I mostly eating canned good food and noodles?
Why was I putting boiling hot water in the bath tub?
Why were my lost friends roaches?
Why was I the one that had to kill the rats,
Why was I telling mommy sorry?
Why was I not up to fashion?
Why was I feeling thought love?
Why was my dad leaving so much?
Why was my mom part time dad full-half time mom?
Why was I asking where are the lights?
Why did my family have to be darker than most nights!

"YOU'RE MY FAITH"

You make me feel love,
You give an opening to say I'm worth more,
You put up with my bad and that shows more,
I never thought to say... but I will always love you
cause' you showed me nothing more!

"EYE SEE"

One must state that ambition is only seen in one's acceptance to self,
Attention is played on focus,
Fascinated on building oneself,
the mental is convinced in its qualities,
view every situation to the physical eye beyond reach,
Knowingly now entertainment of knowledge is where self sits, Opportunist has now blossomed,
From one's pessimistic soul, an obtuse mind,
Considering every command pushed on one's old self was never obeyed, one must be sagacious as in wise,
But to self and ask what changes this I-ness adventure to I,
Projecting awareness to self,
Brings a realization to oneself and it grasps to inform the mind,
(Know True Self),

"SEND OFF"

This is me no more or less... Yes, it is time to give mourning goodbyes,
Grieve well my people from the out to the inside,
I send my love to you from this dark and gloomy sky,
It's so sad I must leave earlier when not so ready to retire,
Not so sure what this sky is going to bring,
But hoping that its PEACE to my spirit and that's a prayer within my great bye,
Tiredness and pain has eaten my body alive,
Must admit I've been ready unconsciously and consciously to say my last hi,
I love you all and wish you so well,
I hope you learned from my lessons that its many better sides,
I leave a wiser man so no need for bad or regretful cries,
To you all my people I ever wrote for and spoke on...I sign off saying I love you whole heartily and a Great-bye!!!

APOLOGETIC FLIPPED WAS SWITCHED

To all who know me as my past or my present mistakes I write this for you. I write this with such compassion, passion, sorrow, pain and shame but with strength from within. To anyone I have ever caused to become a victim due to my ignorance and understanding of life. I grieve over the pain I caused, whosever business I have destroyed or brought my ignorance into. I make no excuses for these actions, but I would love for you to allow me to bring true clarification! I apologize, and I don't use the word sorry wildly or loosely, but I am sorry to you all. For so long I have been faced with such of a disease which can result in loneliness, pain, struggle, neglect of self and everything one comes encounter with. Most of all, it brings oneself complete self-destruction. This disease can have one so numb that it doesn't feel humiliation, shame or disappointment in self.

Well today, I am ashamed by these acts, humiliated and disappointed in myself. Now yes, I know many would say some of these feelings aren't good for oneself, but I have to also come to realization within myself and say enough is enough. Not only am I creating victims and issues for others, I am even creating situational problems for myself pretending like I taste the flavor when I'm so lonely. The only flavor I'm tasting is bittersweet. I want all to know that I am better than my past acts and present mistakes.

I am a man fighting to breathe through such loneliness and distress. Having to walk with a smile that's only good when produced in light and released with night. Due to this vampire of pain that must be fed, as it felt such at the time, not thinking of any way but disease way.

To you all, I am sorry that I have caused such hurt. I was told hurt people can hurt people and now I have gained such insight from experience. Why when one wants love, they choose to abuse and not love? I guess when it seems pain is your pleasure, you roll with the norm and all you feel is the numb.

This disease has corrupted my entire being, mind, body and soul to the point 13 years passed and I've barely flinched or noticed; now if that's not blind, deaf and ignorant. This disease I have now begin to look even more closely into, has not only been passed down, but when I thought or think I got it beat, it defeats the odds with remarkable scores. I have pushed so hard to fight this disease, my people.... Fight after fight after fight and always come to wonder how I haven't beat it yet. One more time then I lift my head up to see I'm back at another 100 losses. Then it came to me, what am I doing fighting such tyrant? Why not just let it win somewhere else? Why not just...why not just let it win the fight? Sometimes letting in to such can be the win. Every great fight wasn't won with a fist, most was with a single thought. That had me in thought which led me to a decision to win back what's rightfully mine. The only vaccine for this disease is strictly self-consciousness. Once again, my first solution is now my last.

    To you Grinell Tyson Jr. I am sincerely sorry, also, to cast such pain and hurt upon you. I apologize for making you so foolish for not helping when I saw you drowning knowing that I know C.P.R.

    And to all who suffered from any of my wrong doings, I swear wholeheartedly that I am sincerely sorry. I say this knowing I'm better than a sorry. I ask you all PLEASE forgive me and everything I have done. See me walk as I do from this day forward and judge no longer my past. With that, just as I asked God, I want you all to know this forgiveness will not go unserved. Thank you!

TAKE THESE TIPS THAT I LEND WITH ALL MY LOVE:

- Learn and study one before you jump into moving their life around or judge their actions.
- Learn their culture and their lifestyle; down to the words they sing and hear the reasons behind it.
- Look at your capabilities and make no false promises.
- Look at yourself and your background; know that everyone is not the same. Listen to the silent cries behind what is being said. Sit down with your child, client etc. And truly hear them; comfort over a meal is sometimes better than sitting in an office.
- Pull out a box of toys and ask which one would you choose and why? No age is too old for this.

- Give some of yourself; don't be scared to put yourself out there. Just understand the lines that you should not cross.
- Ask yourself why you are doing this? Think about the reason you place yourself in the seat you're in. If no great thought with action comes to mind, get up and allow someone else to have that seat.

LAST WORDS

To the ones who are sick and suffering:

Let my words bring greatness in your times of pain and feeling misunderstood. I want you, some of my most important readers, to know that all is possible. Look deep within yourself, learn you (WHO ARE YOU?) and search for that greatness. To the ones stuck in a life that feel there is no other way out. **To my gang member(s), to the ones struggling with addictions, those involved in the street life/love, my ones suffering from depression or heartbreak/pain, those suffering from being a victim and/or trauma.** It is you who I am close with, my circumstances have been some and plenty. It's us who are built with true greatness, for we hold information most classes can't just outright teach. We are thinkers, sometimes that's all we do. In worse case, sometimes a little too much, if you know what I mean. We are made with great hearts so much sometimes we may lose control. I am here to tell you search deep, find your true path because there is one for you and it is where your true wealth lays. These are my words to you. Today may not be great but tomorrow hasn't come, so manage time best as you can to fix and get right what's needed. You are one thought away from making your greatness happen or letting your Mom, Dad, Child or Children, Grandparents and most importantly **yourself** down. I see a King in you! I see a Queen in you! Now it is your turn to turn on that light. You know that light that comes on inside of you, only you feel and know about. They always told me I would go-to jail or be dead or locked back in a mental hospital; when it wasn't said, I assumed their eyes did. But I am here speaking to you hoping and praying with all faith that you too will wake up and allow yourself to live best as you can. So please take a self-inventory, track down what's going on inside of you. And let's start changing some of those old thinking patterns. Change is not always easy, but it is possible. If it was up to most, I might still be taking more medication than love or put some where away from society. If you need help, seek it. There are great people out here willing to give it. There are some resources that can meet your needs and designed for whatever issues you may be going through. All I need is for you to take that first step. I end my message to you with all P.E.A.C.E and LOVE!

Sincerely,

Grinell Tyson Jr.

Want to contact Mr. Tyson? Feel free to email him: frmhoodtoman@gmail.com

~NOTES~

www.ingramcontent.com/pod-product-compliance
Lightning Source LLC
Chambersburg PA
CBHW020904090426
42736CB00008B/486